COMPARATIVE STUDY OF SELECT SHAKESPEAREAN TRAGEDY AND HINDI MOVIES BASED ON THEM

PURNENDU SHEKHAR DUBEY

Contents

Amity University, Mumbai Amity School Of Languages A Study Of Literary Adaption:--

Comparative Study Of Select Shakespearean Tragedy And Hindi Movies Based On Them.

Submitted To:-- Mrs. Manjiree AtulVaidyaHeadofInstitute,AmitySchoolOf Languages

Submitted By:--Purnendu Shekhar Dubey

Roll No.:--01

Course:-- B.A.(H.) English Literature

Semester:-- 06

Dissertation submitted in part ful fill mentin The Requirements of The B.A.(H.)

English Literature, Degree of The Amity University Amity School Of Languages.

ACKNOWLEDGEMENT

I have taken Efforts in This Project. However, It would not have been Possible Without The Kind Support and Help of Many Individuals. I would like to Extend My Sincere Thanks to All of Them.

I'm highly Indebted to Mrs. Manjiree Atul Vaidya for The Guidance and Constant Supervision, as well as, for providing Providing Necessary Information Regarding The Project and Also for Their Support in Completing My Project.

I would like to Express My Gratitude To wards My Mother and Sister for Their Kind Co-Operation and Encouragement, Which Help Mein Completing The Project.

My Thanks and Appreciation also goes to My Colleague in Developing The Project and People, Who have Willingly Helped Me Out with Their Abilities.

CERTIFICATE

This is to Certify, that, Purnendu Shekhar Dubey, A Student of Amity University has Successfully Completed His Project, Titled "Film And Literature" In Our University, With Reference to The Partial Fulfillment of The Requirements of The B.A. English Literature Degree Course.

All Necessary Details were Provided from Our Side for The Establishment of This Project.

We Wish Him The Very Best In All His Future End eavours.

Thanking You,

With Regards,

Amity University

Purnendu Shekhar Dubey

Dr. Manjiree Atul Vaidya

Student Sign

Head Of Institution

Amity School Of Languages

Abstract

Shakespearean tragedies have been aperennial source of inspiration for all film makers across the world. While some attempt transpose the text exactly and recreate the periodon screen, others like Vishal Bharadwaj have their own ways of mixing and matching. This paper will be based on the in depth analysis of the feature Maqbool, which is loosely based on the Shakespearean tragedy of Macbeth. The plot, context and the characters of the film will be analyzed and compared with the original text of the play Macbeth to mark out the similarities and the differences .But the major attempt of the authors is to appreciate the craftsmanship of the director and not to critically analyze it.

CHAPTER I

INTRODUCTION

This great capacity of story-telling or narration by both these arts–literature and film – has, in fact, kept them inseparable. Since the advent of motion pictures more than a century ago, film makers have borrowed extensively from literary sources suchas novels, plays, histories, and biographies, translating words on a page to pictures on a screen and eventually to pictures and sound in movie houses, on Television into Video Cassettes, Video Compact Discs and in other form of advanced technology. Cinema has always been involved, then, in what came to be called 'Adaptation', the transformation of printed works to another medium.

Referring to this intimate relationship between literature and cinema over the last century Brian

McFarlane even talks about "the pervasive nature of The interest in this confluence of two Art Forms. In fact, they have succeeded, as film has now become the premier art form and also the most popular form of entertainment during the last century not only in America but also in other parts of the world. In spite of the rapid growth of the film world into an industry, adaptation has not been discontinued. It is estimated that adaptation srepresent a full third of Hollywood's annual output, that their quality as measured by Academy Awards out number by almost double of films made from original screen plays, and that most of the biggest box-office winner sover the years area daptations.

CHAPTER

INTRODUCTION

[illegible]

Scope And Limitations Of Study

The critical paradigms suggested by most critics, although varying in the terms used to define categories and the range of discussion designated to each category, appear to sharea principle on which the categoryisation is based: the distance the film adaptation keeps from its source literature. How far the film has drifted away from the original text, how different it has become, and as aresult how independent it has become are the governing concerns with those critics who attempt to deliver the discussion on adaptation from the fidelity issue by legitimising the diverse filmic verions. They delimit the fidelity discussion as just one way of looking at film adaptation, even regarding it as the "least interesting" method. Then they investigate the ways in which a novel is transformed by a film, interms of the narrative structure, historical and geographical settings, characters, and soon. They also look at the possibility, that, film can serve as interpretation or commentary. Finally, they suggest a framework to consider nontextual ingredients used in the adaptation process, unique cultural-historical circumstances influencing the making of the particular film. However, such undertakings operate on a great paradox turning the whole discussion back to the very point from which it was purported to have moved away. When empirically applied, each analytical paradigm becomes unable to hold onto its distinctiveness as an apparatus by which a film is re-contextualised. The actual analysis of the film with in any frameworks uggested above basically coincides with the compare-contrast analysis, as the affinity of the film with the original novel becomes the index to choose a framework. It is not the ways in which a film is analysed, but the final judgement conferred on the film, which is based not on the degree of faithfulness but on the mode and the degree of being faithful or unfaithful, that marks out each paradigm. Critics commenting on an adaptation, therefore, ultimately divide into two groups: those who employ one of the paradigms to look for the gap between the film and its source text and those who regard the faithfulness of the film to the novellas the vital factor in adaptation and evaluation of the film. The analyses of a film produced by the critics of both parties can be similar, if not identical, apart from the moments when the film is judgeda 'success' or 'failure'. The success of the film, for one, depends on the ways in which the film sheds a new light on the novel, discovering or adding new meaning, whereas for the other, the success of the film depends on skilful cinematic translation or representation.

LITERATUREREVIEW

Shakespeare has been the subject of study and analysis in different fields. There have been many scholars and writers in many arenas whose attention has been attracted toward him. Not only writers but also director sand screen writers have been interested in Shakespeare's multi-dimensional plays because their adaptation suggests a good way to earn cultural authority. One of the many other remarkable points about the adaptations of William Shakespeare's plays is their modern quality and how they can easily move from their Elizabeth an context to the modern age to talk about what is going on in the contemporary era. According to Naikar, Dryden thinks of Shakespeare as the man with the most comprehensive soul of all poets. Naikar also points that when Carlyle was asked whether he would give up the Indian Empireor Shakespeare, hesaid, 'Indian Empire or no Empire will go, at any rate, someday; but this Shakespeare does not go, he lasts for ever with us. Shakespeare's popularity in India started just since his introduction to this British colony. Shakespeare was in traduced in

India during the age of Johnson and Garrickin 1775 as they ear of the American Independence War. The establishment of the Hindu College in 1816, and the teaching of Shakespeare by distinguished teachers like Richardson had such a great effect on the students' minds that they became interested in Shakespeare criticism and would also act his plays. Actually, scholarship in Shakespeare an works has been supposed as the yardstick of proficiency among the Indian professors and intellectuals. Some of the ways in which Shakespeare's influence has been felt in India include translations, adaptations and plays in Indian languages based on the model of Shakespeare's plays especially since the year 2000 and in 'Bollywood' as the term which refers to the prolific Hindi film industry in Bombay.

Objectives

Every study is conducted with some objective. The present study is taken with an objective :--

•To study the popularity of screen adaptation among viewers.

•To compare and analyse the characterisation, story and content between novels and movies.

•To develop Literary Sensibility.

•To develop Critical Thinking, The Wide Variety to shade The Meaning.

•To link The Film and Literature because They Both are Narrative Expression.

METHODOLOGY

The present study is based on content analysis which is a method for summarizing any form of content by counting various aspects of the content. This enables a more objective evaluation than comparing content based on the impressions of an audience. The content that is analysed can be in any form to begin with, but is often converted into written words before it is analysed.

HYPOTHESIS

In the words of Land berg, “A hypothesis is tentative generalization, the validity of which remains to be tested”. Research Hypotheses is a prediction of the outcome of a study. It is assumption or supposeition by the researcher which may be proved or may be disapproved. The Hypothesis for the present study:

1.Movies are more popular than literature or novels due to heterogeneous audience.

2 .Content is not always similar with that of the script of the movie.

Problem Of Research

1.Audience are not well Reader’s

2.They are Not Expose to Variety of Literary Literary Text because They are Very Much Choice Based.

Novels and Films

As mentioned above, the meeting point of literature and film is their art of story- telling, or narration. The fusion of story and cinema, thus, places film in the continuing tradition of narrative forms such as epic, folk tale, myth and the novel. There are many types of films like documentaries, news films, educational films etc. But movies generally cannote a story film. Films continue that tradition of The Narrative.

Similarities between Novels and Films

Novels are narratives. So also are most of the films. Novel sand films have narrative in common: there counting of a sequence of events. Both of them tell stories about characters or what may be called there counting of a sequence of events where the characters are active participants.

However, sometimes certain characters are found to be quite passive.

Differences between Novels and Films

The major difference between novels and films is that the author uses words but the film-maker uses pictures or images. In a novel a scene is described, in a film a scene is depicted. Though the differences look quite simple externally, they are in fact quite complicated. A writer uses different literary techniques such as narration, description, dialogues, interior monologues, figurative languages in the form of images, metaphors, etc. In a film, the film-maker uses mainly two modes: pictures and sound. These two modes also under goth rough highly complex technical processes. For pictures depend up on ways of shooting, lighting, colours, contrasts, mise-en- scene, actors and acting, and also proper editing. Sound, on the other hand, heavily depend upon verbal language, music, environmental sounds, as well as, special sound effects. On every important difference to be noted is that visual images stimulate our perceptions directly, while written words can do this in directly. Reading about a scene requires a kind of mental translation but viewing a picture of a scene does not. Film is a more direct sensory experience than reading. Besides verbal language, there is also colour, movement and Music.

About Shakespeare:--

Will I am Shakespeare (bapt. 26 April 1564 – 23 April 1616) was an English poet ,playwright, and actor, widely regarded as the greatest writer in the English language and the world 's greatest dramatist . He is often called England's national poet and the "Bard of Avon" (or simply "the Bard") . His extant works, including collaborations, consist of some 39 plays, 154 sonnets, two long narrative poems, and a few other verses, some of uncertain authorship. His plays have been translated into every major living language and areper formed more often than those of any other playwright.

About Vishal Bhardwaj :--

Indian film industry, especially the Bombay Film Industry or better known as Bollywood is the largest film industry as per the total number of films made by it in a single year. It produces films invariety of genre, like action, comedy, romantic, satire, etc. Among these is rious types, adaptation films are also seen now and then in the industry and Vishal Bhardwaj is one of the prominent names in that genre. Post 2000, if one considers the film reviews made by the various film critics and the media agencies, it can be certainly inferred that Vishal Bhardwaj is one director who makes the most out of the adaptation films. Vishal Bhardwaj had been making filmad aptation of classic short stories or novels on regular intervals. Though he is established as a film maker today, Vishal Bhardwaj started his film career as a music director. He recorded his composition in the year 1984 but his success as a music composer came much later with films like Machis in1996, Chachi 420 in 1997 and Satyain 1998. It was in2002, Vishal Bhardwaj made his first film Makdee or Web of the Witch a children comedy horror film.

His debut film made waves and was screed at the Cannes film festival under the Spotlight of India segment. According to an interview published in Hindustan times on December 25th, 2015 , becoming a film maker came as a need more that as a choice. Vishal states, " Thes peed with which I got success, it left me as quickly. After Maachis, I worked on Chachi 420 (1997) and Satya, as a composer .At the same time, because Iused to argue a lot with the directors, people started thinking that I' marrogant. The next two- three years werebad. That time, It realized that If I don't do any thing else, I will be back to where I was. One day, Gulzar saab told me that I can be a good director. I stil l don't know why he said that."But what started as need, made him one of the finest film maker of the country. Soon Vishal was busy making his first adaptation i.e. Shakespeare' Macbeth in a gangster based film named "Maqbool". Vishal accidentally came across an abridged version of Macbeth and connected the basic central theme of ambition and guilt to a contemporary gangster plot. Though the film was not agreat commercial success but it was critically appreciated and ushered a new way of a daptation film in contemporary Indian cinema. Further Bhardwaj made two more films based on the Shakespeare's work. Othello was made into "Omkara" in 2006 was a critical and commercial success and in 2014 "Haider" was released based on Hamlet completing the Shakespeare trilogy. With the acclaim that these films recived Vishal Bhardwaj redefined the way art of cinematic adaptations and made him a kind of authority on Shakespeare work [4] [6]. Not just Shakespeare, Vishal has also made a daptation films on Ruskin Bond's works. He made The Blue Umbrella in 2007 and 7 Khoon Maaf in 2011 based on Bond's The Blue Umbrella and Susanna's Seven Husbandsre spectively.

CHAPTER II

Comparitive of Hamlet And Haider

Bhardwaj has tried to keep the major elements of Hamlet but this hasn't restricted him to change it in a way that is more fathomable to the Indian audience. The most important reason to render the plotis to talk about the same problems and themes. As Hutcheon declares themes are possibly of most importance to plays and, at the same time, the easiest adaptable elements across media. Shakespeare wrote Hamlet to talk about the Renaissance, the period in which he lived and the same happens about Haider which is actually a way for Bhardwaj to talk about a contemporary problem.

There are some similarities and differences between Hamlet and Haider. The first similarity is related to the heroic structure of both the play and movie's plot. According to Hogan (2008), the heroic plot is actually two plots which are linked by connecting the invasion with the usurpation. Specifically, the usurper is often in close contact with the invader. As a result, the most archetypal way of over coming the invader is for the hero to return from exile and lead the defense himself or herself.

One of the most essential features of heroic plots is the necessity of taking action by the hero which results in war and violence as highly attractive features for the Indian audiences. In addition to the same heroic plot structure, both Hamlet and Haider can also be said to share the same romantic plot in which the beloved is from the enemy side and the clash between the two sides separates the lovers (Hogan, 2008, p. 42). Moreover, Hamlet and Haider share the same story line that is the story of a man who is trying to know the truth abou this father's death and avenge it.However, the incidents which he encounters in this route lead to his doubt. Among the other shared points is the use of two letters 'H' and 'A' which are common between Hamlet and Haider; even, the famous lines 'Something is rotten in the state of Denmark' is very much applicable to Kashmir where Haider deals with the political problems.

The other major element of the plot is the significance of Skull. In both Hamlet and Haider, the image of skull is the matically important. As the protagonists speak to the skull, they probe into the philosophy of death. However, the plot has undergone certain changes, too; for example, new soliloquys have been created. Actually, the film makers may reconstruct the soliloquys in many way stomake them fit the movie medium. They may transform them into a verbal or visual dialogue, and even some times into a verbal as well as visual dialogue.

CHAPTER III

Comparative Study Of Macbeth And Maqbool

Macbeth is the shortest of Shakespeare"s tragedies and the simplest in its statements, thou shalt not kill. In the words Coleridge, it contains "no reasonings of equivocal morality, no sophistry of self delusion." With eyes wide open to the hideousness of his offence, a brave, imaginative, and morally sensitive man commits a stealthy murder for gain. The retribution is asappaling as the crime – his soul "sslow death in self – horror degradation, loneliness ,and despair, then his bloody extermination. Macbeth is a story of no moral scruple or compunction. The gory acts of the play, done in satanic haste ,intensifie dy the gothic thrills o fthe witches and surreal elements turn this pay inwards in the end with guilt , hallucination and madness. If ever a play was written for the screen, it was this.Its multiple translations and adaptations make an interesting watch to see how different auteurs have treated Macbeth, Lady Macbeth and the witches. Each interpretation constitutes an exploration between tragedy and melodrama in the misty borderlands of human mind and emotion. Aside from supreme entertainment with various layers and shades of good and evil, ambition and bravery; this filmis also the classic incarnation of the historical fact of the unleashing of the Renaissance spirit– secular, individualistic, self conscious, capitalistic, amoral, questing – upon the traditional Christian moral and social order. "Any director will , consciously or unconsciously, shape the rise and fall of the criminal hero, give it a tone and a context , and if not resolve its paradoxes at least define their terms". This play is also as emiotic delight as it dwells on various semantic renderings of words and builds the theme of misinterpretation juxtaposed with„ equivocation‟ by using doubles of words and oxymoron and doublee ntendres till finally before Macbeth‟s coup de grace the double and equivocate meet in a speech;“ ...and begin, To doubt the equivocation of the fiend, That lies like the truth :... "(Shakespeare, Macbeth 58). And also when he is in a sword battle with Macduff, he asks the people not to trust the witches; “they palter with us in a double sense;” All through the play these double words and equivocation together with lack of moral scruple and the compromised senses more from fear than guilt are the highlight of the play. Shakespeare‟s word play genius elevates the play from trifling with good bad to dealing with the surreal, the fantasmatic and another realm away from the corporeal and earthy; making it less a concern of the morality and more of the viscerality of emotion and fear. And the play opens with these word doubles to confound not just the anti– hero Macbeth but even the audience; “foul and fair a day,” “you should be women, and yet your beards forbid me to interpret that you are so,” “nothing is but what is not,” “wouldst not play false, and yet wouldst wrongly win,” “He‟s here in double trust,” And Macbeth; “wise amazed, temperate and furious, and loyal and neutral,” or “daggers in men ‟ssmiles,” “warranty in the theft which steals itself.” The film Macbeth has various facets as is the thing with Shakespeare‟s poetry and interpretation. Though films try and capture most with their technique and the director‟s vision, still to capture all the facets is difficult. This results in seeing interesting interpretations and translations of the great work a theatre; which could be rankling to some puritans but films showcase a new world where tragic ideas could be introduced into the screenplay with sounds, lights and shadows, acting and sets. These elements combine to work with the subtleties of the poetry they are dealing with.

CHAPTER IV

Comparitive Of Othello And Omkara

Will I am Shakespeare has written on varied topics and his writings have always brought characters to life. One of the famous plays of Shakespeare is Othello tells us about the evils of jealousy in all its forms. The weak are jealous of the strong, the inferiors are jealous of the superiors, but when the seed of jealousy enters a loving relationship, it not only breaks the relationship but some times the consequences can be much dire than one can imagine. The play wa swritten by Shakespeare in 1603 and had varied themes including that of racism, jealousy, love, betrayal ,revenge, and repentance. Though it is often said by many that Othello was not an original play and Shakespeare had written it as an adaptation of the Italian writer Cinthio' stale Un Capitano Moro (A Moorish Captain) from Gli Hecatommithi, which was a collection of one hundred stories. During the lifetime of Shakespeare the rewasno English translation of Cinthio's works but still there are stark similarities between Shakespeare's play and the Italian original rather than any other translation that camelater. However, Shake speare had included many characters in his play but Cinthio had less characters in his tale and Desdemona was the only named character in the original one. Also while Cinthiocon cluded with a moral through Desdemona that European women are not wise while choosing their husbands and regret marrying the temperamental males of other nations, Shakespeare revolved his play around the relationships and the extreme feelings surrounding them. Though Othello was adark play with a tragicending, the characters were handled beautifully with each of the mdistinctly standing from one another. Iago plays an important role in the play being an archetypal villain. In the play he has the biggest share ofdialogues. His angst and evilness can be seen through out the play. He knew the weaknesses and sore points of Othello and played with the measily. Othello wasan egoistic man and Iago cunningly toyed with his ego in a smart way. He brilliantly used Othello's own ego against him self without even giving him a hint. Moreover, if we look into its adaptation into the Hindi movie Omkara, released on 2006, directed by Vishal Bhardwaj, we can see how the characters are completely an imitation of Othello but with an Indian quality and a cultural difference to them. Bhardwaj made Omkara and it was very well received at the boxoffice. It was also a critically acclaimed and awarded movie mainly because it has a rustic look to the story and the language used in the movie had a lot of abuses in Khariboli dialect which attracted the local people. The language was appreciated by every one and it gaveway too ther directors to experiment with the same thing after wards in many other movies. One very interesting thing that Bhardwaj adopted was the names of the characters of the film. While the protagonist was named Omkara, the character of Desdemona was named Dolly, Iago was named Ishwar 'Langda' Tyagi, Emilia was named Indu Tyagi, Cassio was named Keshav 'Kesu Firangi' Upadhyaya, Rodrigo was named Rajan 'Rajju' Tiwari, and Bianca was named Billo. The impressive thing into naming these characters is that each name starts with the same sound as their counterparts in the play. Bhardwaj must have chosen the names cunningly to blend into the adaptation well. The famous actor Ajay Devgan played aimportant role in the movie and his intense acting was just perfect for the character it played. The other praise worthy character of the film was Ishwar 'Langda' Tyagi, played by Saif Ali Khan that was based on the character of Iago from the play. His evil and cunning characterisation brought many accolades from the viewers and the critics both. Although the movie was an adaptation of the play and the language was also changed still there was one of the most important dialogue from the play that was directly translated into Hindi language. In Othello it was Desdemona's father who had spoken this to the moor and in the film it was Dolly's father, which is Desdemona's father in the movie, who spoke the same dialogue. The original lines from the play were, "Look to her Moor, if thou hast eyes to see. She has deceived her father and may thee." It was a dialogue of the utmost importance in the play because this was something that had stuck into Othello's mind which was later on used by Iago. In the movie also, the dialogue painfully hit Omkara and haunted him later. Langda Tyagi used the dialogue to further infuriate Omkara by sowing the seed of jealousy in him. The rustic scenic beauty of the movie had set an Indian mood for the viewers and them elodious song spenned by Gulzar added to the quality of the movie. The lighting of the movie was not very bright from the beginning. It was always dull shade of brown that was splattered on the screen to reflect the picturesque view of the countryside. Th e way situations are developed in the play is being duplicated in the movie as well. The development of the story and the situations are similar and the characters were also growing along with the plot of the movie. Bhardwaj has always been looking into the depth of the movie. His vision while film making is extraordinary. He could read between the lines of the text and subtly incorporate the vital issues of the play in the movie. He basically concentrates on one scene at a time and handles the emotions and their presentations in a very gentle way. The Difficult emotions like, jealousy, guilt, and covetousness has been handled in the movie in a natural way and it is not difficult for the viewers to relate to them. The poetic visuals, dangerous power of jealousy, and conviction in actions in the movies how ed the capability of the director of understanding the darker side of love and relationships. Othello has been famous for the poignant emotions it portray. It is praise worthy that Bhardwaj invoked interest of the audience from an adaptation which showed intense emotions but with an Indian setup and a rustic mood to it. Shakespearean plays are known for their hard hitting reality and tragic endings that beautifully present its characters and their traits. In no way Bhardwaj was behind the famous play wright while sketching his characters and depicting the intense drama on screen. He gave justice to the innocence of Dolly and the slyness of Ishwar equally. Now here could we say that the projection of the characters that were taken from the original text went missing in the movie.

CHAPTER V

Vishal Bhardwaj had shown through his film making that his talent is par excellence. The conversion of the periodic era and the social settings of the original play into Hindi cinema was not an easy task still Bhardwaj emphatically portrayed on the screen the soul of the play not disappointing any Shakespearean fan. Adaptations of literary works into cinema is another art where many filmmakers do not succeed. There are certain similarities between the two mediums but covering up the differences they have, is as kill that note very one can master. When discussing about the similarities of literature and cinema, we can see that there is building of the impression of reality in both. There are many techniques that help an author and a film maker to make their works close to reality in order for the audience to connect themselves. While in a book the writing techniques are the most important one where through words and phrases one can explain different situations and scenic views, but in a movie there are more techniques that can help connect a viewer to it. Some of those techniques include lighting, camera angles, and of course the dialogues. Films are not merely reproduction of reality rather it is a reproduction of the vision of the audience. The audience is always well aware of the fact that what ever they are watching on the screen is a work of fictions till through the cinema to graphic techniques the incidents shown emphatically impose their existence. The manner in which both the medium express their meaning is where the similarities and the differenceslie. When on one hand words are the only medium for a book to convey its meaning, cinema on the other hand has other techniques apart from verbal we can see that dialogues like action, scenic views, lighting, non-verbal cues, and music that could help the audience interpret the meaning of the film in a better way. It is not difficult to understand the fact that audio-visual experience has amore powerful and long lasting effect on a person than that of the written words. Through his trilogy, Bhardwaj has shown the mastery art of film making. The way he projects his characters seem to come straight from the Shakespearean plays but the treatment is truly Indian which helps the audience to connect with them. If this relation of literature and cinema keeps ongoing, Hindi cinema will cross boundaries in excellence with the help of the talented director sit already have, including Bhardwaj who could clearly be seen as the harbinger of international fame to Indian movies based on famous adaptations.

CHAPTER VI

1.https://www.sparknotes.com/shakespeare/hamlet/plot-analysis/

2.https://www.cliffsnotes.com/Literature/h/hamlet/Character-analysis/hamlet

3.https://www.tandfonline.com/doi/full/10.1080/23311983.2016.1260824

4.https://www.en.m.wikipedia.org./wiki/Haider_(film)

5.https://www.researchgate.net/publication/299459476_Haider_dir_by_Vishal_Bhardwaj

6.https://www.Solidpapers.com/Collagepapers/Shakespeare%20macbeth/12276.htm

7.https://www.dreamessays.com/Custumessays/Macbeth/2672.htm

8.https://www.academia.edu/Documents/in/Macbeth

9.htttps://www.cliffsnotes.com/literature/m/Macbeth/Character-analysis/macbeth

10.https://www.Sparknotes.com/Shakespeare/Macbeth

11.https://www.enotes.com/topics/Macbeth/indepth

12.https://www.Solidpapers.com/Collagepapers/Shakespeare%20Othello/12565.htm

13.https://www.cliffsnotes.com/Literature/o/Othello/Character-analysis/Othello

14.https://www.sparknotes.com/Shakespeare/Othello/plot_analysis/

15.https://en.m.wikipedia.org/wiki/Omkara_(2006_film)

16.https://m.hindustantimes.com/india/Omkara/Story-Vok440QiAXZ8Rni0nIL6UK.html

9 798887 170176

Printed by Libri Plureos GmbH in Hamburg,
Germany